ZERO TO TEN

For Frank, SS
For Anna, SN

This edition published in 2003

Publisher: Anna McQuinn
Art Director: Tim Foster
Publishing Assistant: Vikram Parashar

First published in Great Britain in 2001 by Zero To Ten Limited
327 High Street, Slough, Berkshire, SL1 1TX

A CIP catalogue record for this book is available from
the British Library.

ISBN 1-84089-273-0

Printed in Hong Kong

Let's look at
HANDS

Written by
Simona Sideri

Illustrated by
Sheilagh Noble

Look, hands are amazing!

How many fingers?
How many thumbs?

Moles have long broad nails on their front paws.

They are excellent for digging!

Bears have paws
with very long claws.

These are great for
getting at roots and honey.

Seals use their flippers like paddles.

Flippers are super for swimming,
but a little clumsy for walking.

Bats and birds soar
on their wonderful wings.

Octopuses have eight
long tentacles.

They can reach out
to catch prey, and
the suckers underneath
help them grip
tightly onto rocks.

Elephants use their trunks like we use our hands!

Or like a hose
for a cool shower!

Hands are **handy!**

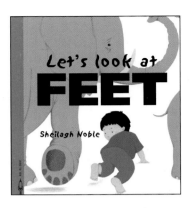

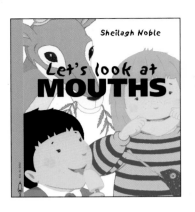

Hardback
ISBN 1-84089-145-9

Paperback
ISBN 1-84089-273-0

Hardback
ISBN 1-84089-144-0

Paperback
ISBN 1-84089-274-9

Hardback
ISBN 1-84089-147-5

Paperback
ISBN 1-84089-276-5

Hardback
ISBN 1-84089-146-7

Paperback
ISBN 1-84089-275-7

"SEARCH FOR THE ROCKET"

ZERO TO TEN publishes quality picture books for children aged between
zero and ten and we have lots more great books about animals!
Our books are available from all good bookstores.

If you have any problems obtaining any title, or would like to receive information about our books, please contact the publishers:
ZERO TO TEN 327 High Street, Slough, Berkshire SL1 1TX Tel: 01753 578 499 Fax: 01753 578 488